Max's
Counting
Adventure

Max's
Counting
Adventure

Steven M Roper

Max's Counting Adventure
Steven M Roper

Through Max's adventure, children can learn about counting, teamwork, and the idea that it's not just about how much you have, but the joy of sharing and working together.

Max the squirrel loved to collect acorns.

One sunny morning, he decided to go on a big adventure to gather as many acorns as he could.

He thought it would be fun to count them along the way.

Max scurried through the forest and found his first acorn.

He picked it up and said, "One! I found one acorn!" He was so excited.

Max kept going, searching under trees and bushes, and soon, he found two more acorns.

"Two, three!" Max giggled. "I have three acorns now!"

As he walked, Max saw his friend Bella, the bunny, hopping by.

She noticed the acorns in his paws. "Max, what are you going to do with all of those acorns?" she asked.

"I'm counting them, Bella! I want to see how many I can collect by the end of the day!" Max explained proudly.

Bella smiled. "That sounds like fun! Can I help?"

Max thought for a moment. He loved counting, but he realized that it might be even more fun to have a friend help.

"Of course, Bella! Let's find more acorns together!"

Bella and Max hopped and scurried through the forest, working as a team.

Soon, they found four acorns near a tall oak tree.

Bella picked them up, and Max counted, "Four, five, six, seven!"

They added them to Max's basket, which was getting heavier.

As they continued, Max and Bella spotted three more acorns hidden in a patch of grass.

Bella collected them carefully, while Max counted aloud, "Eight, nine, ten! We did it, Bella!

We found ten acorns!"

Max's basket was full, and they had reached their goal of collecting ten acorns. But Max was feeling a little tired now.

Bella noticed Max slowing down. "Max, do you think we have enough acorns now?" she asked kindly.

Max thought for a moment. He had wanted to see how many acorns he could collect, but he realized something important.

"Bella, I think we do. But you know what?

It's not just about how many acorns I have. It's about how much fun we had together."

Bella smiled. "That's right! And we worked together as a team!"

Max nodded happily. "Yeah! And we counted all the way to ten! That's a big number!"

Max and Bella sat down by the oak tree and shared their acorns with their forest friends.

Max learned that sometimes, the best part of an adventure isn't just reaching your goal, but enjoying the journey with a friend.